Family Time with God

60 BIBLE-BASED DEVOTIONS FOR PARENTS & KIDS

DAVID AND NAOMI SHIBLEY

BroadStreet
PUBLISHING

BroadStreet Publishing® Group, LLC
Savage, Minnesota, USA
BroadStreetPublishing.com

Family Time with God: 60 Bible-Based Devotions
for Parents and Kids
Copyright © 1981, 2008, 2021 David and Naomi Shibley

978-1-4245-6314-2 (faux leather)
978-1-4245-6315-9 (e-book)

Stock or custom editions of BroadStreet Publishing titles may
be purchased in bulk for educational, business, ministry,
fundraising, or sales promotional use. For information, please
email orders@broadstreetpublishing.com.

Design and typesetting | garborgdesign.com

Printed in China

21 22 23 24 25 5 4 3 2 1

To Tomorrow's Christ-Followers

CONTENTS

WHY JESUS CAME TO EARTH

GOD'S SPIRIT

HOW TO MAKE GOD HAPPY

HOW TO LIVE

IMPORTANT WORDS

A WORD TO PARENTS AND GRANDPARENTS

This book is the result of our own needs as new parents. When our sons were young, several excellent family devotional materials were available; however, we searched high and low for a book that combined Scripture memorization, brief stories, simple catechisms, conversation starters, and short prayers, all while reinforcing the basic truth of the gospel. We also needed a devotional resource that featured a workable, flexible system. In your hands is the book for which we had searched. And through our frustrations, failures, and victories, we arrived at five basic principles that we're convinced are valid:

Brevity is key. When it comes to communicating faith to young children, several brief doses are usually best. Our adult attention spans are sometimes short but imagine how much shorter they are in children! For this reason, we've kept each session no longer than five minutes. The strength of family devotions lies not in length but consistency.

Repetition is vital. The parents of Israel were commanded by God to reinforce his truth to their children at four natural points during the day: "These words which I command you today shall be in your heart; you shall teach them diligently to your children, and shall talk of them when you sit in your house, when you walk by the way, when you lie down, and when you rise up" (Deuteronomy 6:6–7). The repetition of a specific truth at spaced intervals produces solid results, so we've strategically divided the book into seven sections composed of several smaller sessions. Each session presents one major truth that is designed to be read and reinforced for one week.

Families today are incredibly busy, and we don't "walk by the way" anymore. Most of us drive—to school, soccer practice, or other activities, which is another reason we kept these devotions brief. The verses and key truths can be repeated and reinforced in the daily routines of dining together, traveling together, getting ready for the day, and ending the day.

Teach the essentials. We live in a culture that has cut loose from its Judeo-Christian moorings and is consequently drowning in a sea of subjectivism. However, we know that right living stems from right thinking, which is why the content of these devotions is strong in basic Christian doctrine, such as the Ten Commandments, the Beatitudes, and the Apostles' Creed. The Ten Commandments provide our children the stability and direction that they need and deserve. Likewise, the Beatitudes form a basis for a life-affirming system of ethics and behavior, and the Apostles' Creed is a clear summary of Christian belief and one of the most universal of all the church's statements.

Perhaps no one can be more successful in relating foundational concepts to children than those who love them most, so parents and grandparents are encouraged to interject personal insight and applicable experiences while journeying through this book. For example, in the session "God Made You," you may wish to share with your children how you prepared for them even before birth. Share how you prayed for them and how God lovingly answered your prayers. These are opportunities for you to impart your Christian faith to your children or grandchildren.

We are strong advocates of child evangelism since both of us came to faith in Christ early in life. We firmly believe it is never too early to share the gospel with children. Sadly, many children today are more familiar with Thor than they are with Jesus. Our children suffer not from overexposure to Jesus but underexposure to him. That's why this book is unapologetically evangelistic in tone.

Jesus said, "Let the little children come to Me, and do not forbid them; for of such is the kingdom of God" (Mark 10:14).

Memorize Scripture. King David affirmed, "Your word I have hidden in my heart, that I might not sin against You" (Psalm 119:11). We're grateful for the many translations of the Bible that are available today, and we encourage you to use the translation of your preference when memorizing verses. We grew up with the King James Version of the Bible, and that translation provided continuity and familiarity for us when relaying Scripture from our generation to that of our sons. But more important than the translation you choose is the imperative of planting God's Word into the hearts and minds of children.

Impart life! Books provide information, but that's not enough. Only Jesus Christ can give spiritual life. Our children and grandchildren will see him, or fail to see him, as they witness our lives. We must be ever mindful that the goal of all our instruction is for those children whom we love to experience a vibrant, living relationship with Jesus as their Savior and Lord.

We've known firsthand the mixture of duty and despair that so many Christian parents feel concerning family devotions, but this practice is a small investment that yields valuable, eternal dividends. And when we first began using the contents of this book in our family time, the results were so encouraging that we simply had to share them.

Our two sons were little boys when this book was first published. Now they are grown, married, and servants of Jesus Christ. We've also welcomed two beautiful Christian daughters-in-law and five grandchildren, and we continue to learn how to improve the efficacy of our family devotions.

We're grateful for the overwhelming response this book has received throughout the years. Now we pray it will bring blessing to you and your family for years to come.

David and Naomi Shibley

What God Is Like

LET'S REMEMBER

*In the beginning God created
the heavens and the earth.*

GENESIS 1:1

LET'S LISTEN

Look up! God made the sun, moon, stars, and sky. Look around! God made the trees, plants, and animals. He made pretty flowers. He made food in our gardens. He made the oceans and rivers and fish in the sea. God made people too. He created the entire world. He made everything out of nothing.

Everything God made is for his glory. That means that everything everywhere was made to please God.

LET'S ANSWER

Question: Who made everything?
Answer: God made everything.

> ## LET'S TALK ABOUT IT
>
> Name some things God made.

LET'S PRAY TOGETHER

Thank you, God, for making everything beautiful.
Help me take good care of your world. Amen.

*Use these prayers as guides. We also suggest parents and grandparents encourage their children in spontaneous expressions of prayer and praise.

LET'S REMEMBER

I will praise You, for I am fearfully and wonderfully made.

PSALM 139:14

LET'S LISTEN

After God made the world, he made a man named Adam and a woman named Eve. All the people of the world came from them, including you.

God made people so that they could love him. We call this "being made in God's image." This makes people more important than anything else God made.

Although we are all made in God's image, no one else in the world is like you. God made you special, and he has something important for you to do.

LET'S ANSWER

Question: Who made you?
Answer: God made me.

Question: Why are people so important?
Answer: Because people are made in God's image.

LET'S TALK ABOUT IT

You can see yourself in a mirror. Who is reflected in the mirror? What do you think it means to be made in God's image?

LET'S PRAY TOGETHER

Thank you, God, for making me. Thank you for my body. Thank you for my mind. Thank you that I can know you. I'm glad you have given me something important to do with my life. Help me to live my life for you. Amen.

LET'S REMEMBER

*Go therefore and make disciples of all the nations,
baptizing them in the name of the Father
and of the Son and of the Holy Spirit.*

MATTHEW 28:19

LET'S LISTEN

There is one God who exists forever. He has always been and always will be. God is a Trinity. *Trinity* means "three in one." God the Father, God the Son, and God the Holy Spirit are present with you every day to help you.*

God the Father loves all the people of the world very much. So, he sent his Son, Jesus, from heaven to be born as a baby on earth. Jesus died to save us from our sins, and when he returned to heaven, he sent his Holy Spirit to stay with us. The Holy Spirit guides the church. He lives inside all true Christians.

LET'S ANSWER

Question: What does *trinity* mean?
Answer: Trinity means "three in one."

Question: What three persons make up the one true God?
Answer: God the Father, God the Son, and God the Holy Spirit are the three persons in one true God.

LET'S TALK ABOUT IT

List one or two things that Jesus did to show us what his Father is like.

LET'S PRAY TOGETHER

Dear God, you are the one true God. I love you, Father. I love you, Jesus. I love you, Holy Spirit. Amen.

*While no illustration fully describes the mystery of the Trinity, parents may want to use the analogy of water, ice, and steam to help older children understand the concept of three in one. This can be done by putting ice cubes beside a cup of steaming hot water and explaining that water exists in three forms: solid, liquid, and gas. Likewise, God is three persons: the Father, the Son (Jesus), and the Holy Spirit.

God Is Love

LET'S REMEMBER

God is love.

1 JOHN 4:8

LET'S LISTEN

How do you feel toward a person who makes fun of you or hits you? It's hard to love someone like that, isn't it? But God the Father loves everyone in the world. God loves us even when we don't love and obey him. It is a sin not to love and obey God, and God must punish sin.

God loves you. You are very special to him. The Father loves you so much that he sent his Son Jesus to die for you. That's how you can know he loves you. The Bible says, "God demonstrates His own love toward us, in that while we were still sinners, Christ died for us" (Romans 5:8).

God loves us so much he was willing to be punished in our place. This would be like you asking to take the punishment in place of a brother, sister, or friend who did something wrong. Do you see how much God loves you?

LET'S ANSWER

Question: How do you know God the Father loves you?

Answer: I know the Father loves me because he sent Jesus to die for me.

LET'S TALK ABOUT IT

Some people think God doesn't love them. How do we know he does love them?

LET'S PRAY TOGETHER

Thank you, God, for loving me. Thank you for sending Jesus to die for me. This shows me how much you love me. Amen.

God Is Holy

LET'S REMEMBER

*As He who has called you is holy,
you also be holy in all your conduct.*

1 PETER 1:15

LET'S LISTEN

God is like no one else. He is holy because he
thinks and does only what is right. God wants us
to be holy too. That means he wants us to belong
to him and to love and obey him. Instead of
thinking bad thoughts, he wants us to think good
thoughts. Instead of doing wrong things, he wants
us to do what is right and good. God can help us
do the right things. God is happy when we ask
him to make us holy, and we are happy too.

LET'S ANSWER

Question: What does it mean to be holy?
Answer: To be holy means to belong to God and to love and obey him.

LET'S TALK ABOUT IT

God has never done anything wrong. This is because he is holy. He wants to make us holy too. In what situations might you need God's help to be holy? For example, what should you do if someone says mean things about you?

LET'S PRAY TOGETHER

Thank you, God, for being holy. I'm glad that you think and do only what is right. Help me to live like that too. Amen.

God Is Our Father

LET'S REMEMBER

As many as received Him [Jesus], to them He gave the right to become children of God.

JOHN 1:12

LET'S LISTEN

God created everyone, but not every person has God for his or her heavenly Father. You see, when someone invites Jesus into their life, God becomes their Father in heaven. You may have a father living here on earth. How wonderful that we can have God as our Father too! He loves us even more than any father here on earth. He is always able to give us what we need, and he will take care of us perfectly.

LET'S ANSWER

Question: When does God become your Father?
Answer: God becomes my Father when I receive Jesus into my life.

LET'S TALK ABOUT IT

How do we know that God is a good Father?

LET'S PRAY TOGETHER

We read in Matthew 6:9–13 that Jesus taught us
to pray in this way:

> *Our Father in heaven,*
> *Hallowed be Your name.*
> *Your kingdom come,*
> *Your will be done,*
> *On earth as it is in heaven.*
> *Give us this day our daily bread,*
> *And forgive us our debts,*
> *As we forgive our debtors.*
> *And do not lead us into temptation,*
> *But deliver us from the evil one.*
> *For Yours is the kingdom*
> *and the power*
> *and the glory forever.*
> *Amen.*

God's Son Is Jesus

LET'S REMEMBER

Simon Peter answered and said, "You are the Christ, the Son of the living God."

MATTHEW 16:16

LET'S LISTEN

Jesus is God, and he is also a man.* This is difficult to understand, and even adults can't explain it. They can only say that the Bible teaches it. The Bible calls this a "mystery."

God arranged to have Jesus born as any other baby and to grow up the same way you are growing up. Since Jesus is a man, he was sometimes tired and hungry. But since Jesus is God, he never did anything that was sinful or wrong. Jesus is God's special-born Son who lived forever with his Father in heaven before coming to earth. The Bible calls him God's "only begotten Son" (John 3:16). Still today, Jesus is God and man all at once.

LET'S ANSWER

Question: Who is God's special-born Son?
Answer: Jesus is God's special-born Son.

LET'S TALK ABOUT IT

Name some ways that Jesus is special and like no one else.

LET'S PRAY TOGETHER

Thank you, Jesus, for showing me what your Father is like. I know God the Father loves me because you love me, and you are God and man, both at once. I believe that you were special-born from heaven, that you were born on earth, and that you are the Son of the living God. Amen.

*Read Matthew 1:23; Romans 5:17

LET'S REMEMBER

*When He, the Spirit of truth has come,
He will guide you into all truth.*

JOHN 16:13

LET'S LISTEN

We call God's Spirit the Holy Spirit. The Holy Spirit lets people know they need Jesus in their lives. After a person becomes a follower of Jesus, the Holy Spirit comes and lives inside him and makes him able to be the kind of person that makes God happy.

The Bible calls these good things "the fruit of the Spirit" (Galatians 5:22–23). The Holy Spirit gives special gifts to Christians. He also helps them live for Jesus and tell others about him.

LET'S ANSWER

Question: Who makes people know they need Jesus in their lives?
Answer: The Holy Spirit.

Question: Who makes Christians able to live a life that pleases God?
Answer: The Holy Spirit makes Christians able to live a life that pleases God.

LET'S TALK ABOUT IT

What do you need the Holy Spirit to help you do?

LET'S PRAY TOGETHER

Holy Spirit, you are God, just as Jesus is God and the heavenly Father is God. Help me to know when you speak to me and help me to obey you always.
Amen.

God's Rules for a Good Life

No Other Gods

LET'S REMEMBER

You shall have no other gods before Me.

EXODUS 20:3

LET'S LISTEN

Long before Jesus was born, God gave rules to Moses for the people of Israel to obey. We call these rules the Ten Commandments. When we obey God's commands, we make God happy.

The first rule commands us to worship and serve God alone. No other person or thing should take first place in our lives, which only God deserves. We must never let anyone or anything become more important to us than God.

LET'S ANSWER

Question: Who should be most important in your life?

Answer: God should be most important in my life.

LET'S TALK ABOUT IT

What are some things that could become more important to us than God if we let them?

LET'S PRAY TOGETHER

Dear God, I will worship and serve you alone. May nothing ever become more important to me than you. Amen.

LET'S REMEMBER

You shall not make for yourself a carved image.

EXODUS 20:4

LET'S LISTEN

Some people don't worship the true and living God. They worship gods they make themselves—statues of wood, stone, or metal. These statues are not the real God. They cannot hear or answer when people pray to them. They are false gods. The Bible calls them "graven images" or "idols."

But an idol can be anything that becomes more important to us than God. Even other people might become idols to us. We must not have any idols in our lives.

LET'S ANSWER

Question: What is an idol?

Answer: An idol is anything that is more important to me than God.

LET'S TALK ABOUT IT

What are some things that could become idols in your life?

LET'S PRAY TOGETHER

Dear God, you are the true and living God. May I never have any idol in my life. I will love and serve you with my whole heart. Amen.

LET'S REMEMBER

*You shall not take the name
of the Lord your God in vain.*

EXODUS 20:7

LET'S LISTEN

When people use God's name without proper
respect, they are taking his name in vain. People
sometimes curse, using the name of God the
Father or Jesus, his Son. God clearly commands
us not to do this. God warns us that those who
take his name in vain will one day be punished
for it.

When we speak God's name, we must always
remember that he is the almighty God, the ruler
of heaven and earth. His name is always to be
spoken with honor and respect.

LET'S ANSWER

Question: What does it mean to take God's name in vain?

Answer: When people speak God's name without proper respect, they are taking his name in vain.

LET'S TALK ABOUT IT

How can we make sure we never take God's name in vain?

LET'S PRAY TOGETHER

Help me, God, to be careful of what I say. May I always respect and honor you and your name in all that I say and do. Amen.

LET'S REMEMBER

Remember the Sabbath day,
to keep it holy.

EXODUS 20:8

LET'S LISTEN

God rested on the seventh day after he had created the heavens, the earth, and Adam and Eve. He has told us, too, to take one day of rest each week.

Sunday is the day we set aside for God. Most Christians worship together on Sundays to celebrate the day that Jesus rose from the dead. This is our special day for the Lord. On that day, we should worship him, remember all the wonderful things he has done, and rest with our family.

LET'S ANSWER

Question: How can you keep Sunday holy?

Answer: I can keep Sunday holy by worshiping God, remembering all the wonderful things he has done, and resting with my family.

LET'S TALK ABOUT IT

What should our family do to keep the Sabbath day holy?

LET'S PRAY TOGETHER

Dear God, help me to remember to make Sunday a special day just for you. Amen.

LET'S REMEMBER

*Honor your father and your mother,
that your days may be long upon the land.*

EXODUS 20:12

LET'S LISTEN

God gave us parents because he loves us. God uses parents to bring us into his world, to protect us, and to help us love and obey God.

We honor our parents by obeying them. We should always be respectful of them and do what they say. We should try to please our parents by doing what we know is right. This pleases God too. God promises a long life to those who honor their parents.

LET'S ANSWER

Question: How do you honor your parents?
Answer: I honor my parents by obeying them and respecting them.

LET'S TALK ABOUT IT

What are some ways you can show that you honor your parents?

LET'S PRAY TOGETHER

Thank you, God, for my parents. Help me to always respect them and obey them. Amen.

LET'S REMEMBER

You shall not murder.

Exodus 20:13

LET'S LISTEN

Every person is very special to God. Even before we were born, God knew about us, cared about us, and loved us. Since God gave us life, we should never plan to harm or take life away, ours or anyone else's.

We are to respect our own lives and the lives of others. God gave every person the great gift of life. We are to protect this wonderful gift.

LET'S ANSWER

Question: Who gave you life?
Answer: God gave me life.

Question: How should you treat this gift of life?
Answer: I should thank God for life, respect life, and protect life.

LET'S TALK ABOUT IT

What are some ways you can show respect for your own life and for the lives of others?

LET'S PRAY TOGETHER

Thank you, God, for my life and for the lives of others. May I always respect and protect the lives of all people. Amen.

LET'S REMEMBER

You shall not commit adultery.

Exodus 20:14

LET'S LISTEN

God loves families very much, and he wants families to be happy. So he gave us rules that teach us how to do the right thing. One rule is that people who are married should keep their promises to love and honor each other.

Adultery is when a husband or wife lives with someone who is not the person he or she married. This makes many people sad. God says, "Don't!"

How happy we are when we obey God's rules! God is happy with us, and we are happy with ourselves.

LET'S ANSWER

Question: Why should people never commit adultery?

Answer: People should never commit adultery because God commands us not to commit adultery. He knows it makes many people sad.

LET'S TALK ABOUT IT

When you grow up, God may want you to get married. If he does, he will want you to love and live with the person you marry for the rest of your life. That means loving that person even when he or she is mean or selfish. Who loves us that way? How can we learn to love others, no matter what they do or say to us?

LET'S PRAY TOGETHER

Dear God, I pray that you will keep me pure in my thoughts and in my body. If you want me to marry one day, give me a happy Christian home in which we love and serve you. Amen.

LET'S REMEMBER

You shall not steal.

Exodus 20:15

LET'S LISTEN

Stealing is taking something that belongs to someone else. If someone steals something of yours, you feel sad. It may be something you liked very much or something you needed. When someone takes something that isn't theirs, God sees it, and he is not pleased.

Stealing is against God's law. It is sin. It is also against the laws of our country, and it hurts other people. So never take anything that does not belong to you, no matter how small.

LET'S ANSWER

Question: What is stealing?
Answer: Stealing is taking something that belongs to someone else.

LET'S TALK ABOUT IT

Why is it wrong to steal? What can happen to people who steal?

LET'S PRAY TOGETHER

Dear God, help me be careful with what belongs to others. May I never take anything that is not mine.
Amen.

Tell the Truth

LET'S REMEMBER

*You shall not bear false witness
against your neighbor.*

Exodus 20:16

LET'S LISTEN

To bear false witness means to say something that isn't true. It is lying. Sometimes people lie to get others in trouble. Sometimes people lie because they are afraid to tell the truth. God commands us not to lie. It is never right.

God always wants us to tell the truth, and it is important to him. Jesus said, "I am...the truth" (John 14:6). When we go his way, we tell the truth. People can count on what we say. This brings God joy. It brings us joy too.

LET'S ANSWER

Question: What does it mean to bear false witness?
Answer: To bear false witness means to say something that isn't true.

LET'S TALK ABOUT IT

Sometimes it might seem like it would be easier to tell a lie than to tell the truth. When are some of those times? Remember that even in those times we should tell the truth. Why is that true?

LET'S PRAY TOGETHER

Dear God, help me to always tell the truth even if I want to lie. Amen.

You Shall Not Covet

LET'S REMEMBER

You shall not covet.

Exodus 20:17

LET'S LISTEN

"I want *his* toys!" Have you ever heard someone say that? That's an example of what the Bible calls "coveting." Coveting is wanting something that belongs to someone else, and it often leads to stealing. Instead of coveting, we should thank God for what we already have. That is what we call "gratitude." We should also be happy for other people and what they have.

LET'S ANSWER

Question: What is coveting?

Answer: Coveting is wanting something that belongs to someone else.

LET'S TALK ABOUT IT

Name some items that people sometimes covet.

LET'S PRAY TOGETHER

Thank you, God, for everything you have given me. Help me not to wish for anything that belongs to someone else. Amen.

Why Jesus Came to Earth

LET'S REMEMBER

*For all have sinned and fall short
of the glory of God.*

Romans 3:23

LET'S LISTEN

Adam and Eve disobeyed God in the garden of Eden, and people have been disobeying God ever since. When we do not obey God, we are sinning. Sometimes we sin by what we think. Sometimes we sin by what we do. Sometimes we sin by not doing the things we should do.

God hates sin. It forces people to live away from him. Just think how much God loves us that he does not want us to live without him. He sent his own Son, Jesus, to take the punishment we deserved for our sins. Our sins are forgiven when we turn away from them and ask Jesus into our lives.

LET'S ANSWER

Question: What is sin?
Answer: Sin is not obeying God.

Question: Has everybody sinned?
Answer: Romans 3:23 says, "All have sinned."

LET'S TALK ABOUT IT

What are some ways that people don't obey God?

LET'S PRAY TOGETHER

Thank you, God, for loving me even though I have sinned against you. Thank you for sending Jesus to take the punishment for my sins. Amen.

LET'S REMEMBER

For God so loved the world He gave His only begotten Son, that whoever believes in Him should not perish but have everlasting life.

JOHN 3:16

LET'S LISTEN

God the Father loves all people. When he looked down on the earth and saw that all of the people were disobeying him, he still loved them! He doesn't want anyone to die and be away from him forever. So God sent Jesus, his eternal Son, to pay for our sins.

Jesus was God's special-born Son. Jesus came to earth as a baby—just like you. He was born in a stable where animals lived in a little town called Bethlehem. God was his Father, and Mary was Jesus' mother. God chose Joseph, Mary's husband, to help care for Jesus when he was a child. An angel told Joseph, "You shall call His name Jesus, for He will save His people from their sins" (Matthew 1:21).

LET'S ANSWER

Question: Why did God send Jesus to earth?

Answer: Because God loved us so much, he sent his Son to pay for our sins.

LET'S TALK ABOUT IT

What made Jesus such a special baby?

LET'S PRAY TOGETHER

Thank you, Jesus, for coming all the way from heaven. Thank you for being born as a little baby. I'm glad you know what it's like to be my age too.

Amen.

LET'S REMEMBER

*Jesus increased in wisdom and stature,
and in favor with God and men.*

LUKE 2:52

LET'S LISTEN

When Jesus was a child, he grew up just like you are growing up right now. He became wiser as he grew older, and his body became bigger and stronger too. Jesus loved his Father in heaven, and he loved other people. Jesus enjoyed being with other children and liked to go with Mary and Joseph to the temple to worship God, his Father. God was pleased with Jesus.

Because Jesus grew just as you are growing, he knows what it is like to be your age. You can always talk to Jesus, and he will always understand.

LET'S ANSWER

Question: How did Jesus grow as a child?
Answer: Jesus grew in his mind and in his body.
He also grew in favor with God and people.

LET'S TALK ABOUT IT

Does Jesus understand what it's like to be
your age? Why?

LET'S PRAY TOGETHER

*Thank you, Jesus, that you know what it's like to be
my age. Help me to grow as you did. Amen.*

Jesus Did Wonderful Things

LET'S REMEMBER

Jesus went about all Galilee, teaching in their synagogues, preaching the gospel of the kingdom, and healing all kinds of sickness and all kinds of disease among the people.

MATTHEW 4:23

LET'S LISTEN

Jesus did many wonderful things. People loved to listen to him. He told them the good news that what they had waited to see for so long was now here. God's Son, their Savior, had come.

How exciting it was when Jesus came to town! Jesus performed many miracles. A miracle is something only God can do. He helped blind people to see. People who couldn't walk could suddenly walk again. Many people felt sad and afraid, but Jesus took their fear away and made them happy again. When Jesus touched people, they were never the same.

LET'S ANSWER

Question: Jesus did many miracles. What is a miracle?

Answer: A miracle is something only God can do.

LET'S TALK ABOUT IT

Name some of the wonderful things that Jesus did while he was on earth. Name some wonderful things that Jesus is still doing today.

LET'S PRAY TOGETHER

Thank you, Jesus, for caring about people. I'm glad that you care when we are hurt, sad or afraid. I'm glad that you can change us and make us well, happy, and not afraid. Amen.

LET'S REMEMBER

Christ died for our sins according to the Scriptures, and...He was buried, and...He rose again the third day according to the Scriptures.

1 Corinthians 15:3–4

LET'S LISTEN

Jesus never did anything wrong. Sadly, some people didn't like what he was saying and doing, so they made plans to kill him. They arrested Jesus and brought him to Pilate, the Roman ruler, and Pilate said he did not believe Jesus had done anything wrong. But the people yelled, "Crucify him!" Pilate listened to the people and sent Jesus off to die at the hands of the soldiers.

Jesus said, "Father, forgive them, for they do not know what they do" (Luke 23:34). Just before he died, Jesus cried out, "It is finished!" (John 19:30).

Jesus took the full punishment for all our sins when he died on the cross. He died for people everywhere, including you.

LET'S ANSWER

Question: What did Jesus mean when he said, "It is finished!"?

Answer: When he said, "It is finished," Jesus meant that he had made the full payment for all our sins.

LET'S TALK ABOUT IT

It looked like the devil had won when Jesus died on the cross. But he didn't win. Jesus won, and so did we. Why is that true?

LET'S PRAY TOGETHER

Dear Jesus, you love me so much more than I could ever understand. Thank you for dying for me. Thank you for taking the punishment for my sins. Amen.

LET'S REMEMBER

I am He who lives, and was dead,
and behold, I am alive forevermore.

REVELATION 1:18

LET'S LISTEN

Three days after Jesus died, a small group of women went to his tomb. They were amazed to see an angel standing there. The angel said, "He is not here; for He is risen, as He said" (Matthew 28:6). The women ran to tell Jesus' followers, the disciples, this wonderful news. At first, the disciples didn't believe the women, so Peter and John ran to the tomb to see for themselves. But Jesus was not there. It was true! He had risen just as he had promised.

Jesus is still alive today. All power has been given to him. He is the mighty ruler of heaven and earth. Death could not hold him. He broke free! Jesus said, "Because I live, you will live also" (John 14:19).

LET'S ANSWER

Question: Is Jesus alive today?
Answer: Jesus is alive today! "I am He who lives, and was dead, and behold, I am alive forevermore" (Revelation 1:18).

LET'S TALK ABOUT IT

Because Jesus rose from the dead, what will happen to his followers when they die?

LET'S PRAY TOGETHER

Dear Jesus, I'm glad I don't worship someone who is dead and cannot hear me. Many people in the world pray to false gods like that. I'm thankful you are alive! You really hear me when I talk to you. Because you live forever, I can live forever too.
Amen.

LET'S REMEMBER

If I go and prepare a place for you,
I will come again and receive you to Myself;
that where I am, there you may be also.

JOHN 14:3

LET'S LISTEN

Jesus promised that one day he would come back to earth. When he returns, he won't come as a little baby. This time he will come as the mighty King of kings and Lord of lords. People who do bad things will no longer be in control. There will be peace in all the world. Children won't be afraid anymore. Jesus will rule the earth with his great love.

When this happens, loud voices in heaven will say, "The kingdoms of this world have become the kingdoms of our Lord and of His Christ, and He shall reign forever and ever!" (Revelation 11:15). What a wonderful time that will be!

LET'S ANSWER

Question: Who will one day rule over the earth?
Answer: Jesus will one day rule over the earth.

LET'S TALK ABOUT IT

What do you think it will be like when Jesus rules over the earth?

LET'S PRAY TOGETHER

Thank you, Lord Jesus, that one day you will return to rule over the whole world. I'm glad I know that one day you will make everything right. Amen.

LET'S REMEMBER

I am the way, the truth, and the life.
No one comes to the Father except through Me.

JOHN 14:6

LET'S LISTEN

There are many false religions in the world. They were started by people, not by God. False religions do not believe the truth about Jesus. They don't believe that Jesus is the only person who is both God and man together. Only Jesus died to take the punishment for our sins. Only Jesus rose from the dead, and only Jesus will return one day for all those who believe in him and love him.

Many sincere people try to reach God without Jesus. But Jesus said he is the only way to God. We cannot get to heaven without his Son, Jesus Christ, who said, "I am the door. If anyone enters by Me, he will be saved" (John 10:9).

Since Jesus is the only way to heaven, the church sends missionaries all over the world to tell people this important truth. The missionaries tell people the good news that God sent his Son to die for them and to bring them to his kingdom. If those people believe in Jesus, they will live forever with God (John 3:16).

LET'S ANSWER

Question: Who is the only way to God and heaven?

Answer: Jesus is the only way to God and heaven.

LET'S TALK ABOUT IT

Since Jesus is the only way to God and heaven, how should we feel about those who haven't heard the good news about Jesus? (Read Romans 1:14–16.)

LET'S PRAY TOGETHER

Thank you, Jesus, for opening the way to God for everyone who puts their trust in you. You are the way to God and to heaven. Amen.

LET'S REMEMBER

If you confess with your mouth the Lord Jesus and believe in your heart that God has raised Him from the dead, you will be saved…For "whoever calls on the name of the Lord shall be saved."

ROMANS 10:9, 13

LET'S LISTEN

We have learned that Jesus is God's special-born Son who never sinned but took the punishment for our sins when he died on the cross. He rose from the dead and will one day return to earth to rule forevermore. We also learned that Jesus is the only way to heaven.

It's important to know *about* Jesus, but it's even more important for you to *know* him personally, like a friend. You can know Jesus by turning away from your sins and asking him to forgive you and rule your life.* The Bible calls this being "saved" or "born again."

If you choose to invite Jesus into your life, you become God's child and a part of his family. The

Bible says, "As many as received Him, to them He gave the right to become children of God, to those who believe in His name" (John 1:12).

LET'S ANSWER

Question: How can you know Jesus?
Answer: I can know Jesus by turning from my sins and asking him into my life.

LET'S TALK ABOUT IT

Jesus waits for you to ask him into your life. Will you turn away from your sins and invite Jesus into your heart?

LET'S PRAY TOGETHER

If you would like to welcome Jesus into your life, say a prayer like this:

Lord Jesus, thank you for dying for me. I believe you are the Son of God and that you rose from the dead. I'm sorry for my sins. I turn away from them now and turn to you. I trust you alone to get to heaven. I take you now as my own Savior. I will follow you as my Lord for the rest of my life. Thank you for hearing my prayer, forgiving my sins, and coming into my life just as you promised. Amen.

If you prayed that prayer, welcome to God's won-derful family! You have received Jesus, and he has received you. Now you can know Jesus even better.

*You will want to be sensitive to your child's readiness and to the Holy Spirit's leading as you read this devotion, as it will be a meaningful time if your child experiences a spiritual new birth. Avoid having the child simply recite the prayer without a sincere declaration of faith in Christ. If your child has already received Christ or does not under-stand the significance of this act, then modify the *Let's Talk About It* and *Let's Pray Together* portions.

LET'S REMEMBER

He is also able to save to the uttermost those who come to God through Him, since He always lives to make intercession for them.

HEBREWS 7:25

LET'S LISTEN

After Jesus rose from the dead, he stayed on earth for forty days. During that time, he told his disciples that he would have to return to heaven but would send the Holy Spirit in his place to help them and teach them. Jesus also told the disciples to tell everyone the wonderful news about what he had done for them and to teach people everything he had taught them. The Holy Spirit would help them with this big task.

After Jesus told the disciples all of these things, he returned to heaven, where he sat next to God. From that time until now, Jesus has been asking God the Father to bless all those who have believed in him. Just think: if you belong to Jesus, then he is talking to God about you!

LET'S ANSWER

Question: What is Jesus doing right now in heaven?

Answer: Jesus is praying for those who believe in him.

LET'S TALK ABOUT IT

It's so good to know that Jesus is on our side, defending us and praying for us. What do you think Jesus talks about to God the Father?

LET'S PRAY TOGETHER

Dear Jesus, I'm glad that you continue to care about us. You cared for people while you were on earth, and you still care for us now that you're in heaven. Thank you for talking to God about everyone who believes in you. Amen.

LET'S REMEMBER

I will both lie down in peace, and sleep;
For You alone, O Lord, make me dwell in safety.

PSALM 4:8

LET'S LISTEN

It is easy to feel afraid sometimes since there are
so many things about the world that you may not
understand just yet. But the Lord Jesus protects
you. Even if others hurt you, Jesus cares for you.
He will comfort you and always be with you. The
shepherd boy, David, knew the Lord would protect him. He wrote:

The Lord is my shepherd;
I shall not want…
He restores my soul;
He leads me in the paths of righteousness
for His name's sake.
Yea, though I walk through
the valley of the shadow of death,
I will fear no evil;
for You are with me;

Your rod and Your staff, they comfort me…
Surely goodness and mercy shall follow me
all the days of my life;
and I will dwell in the house of the Lord
forever. (Psalm 23)

LET'S ANSWER

Question: Why don't you need to be afraid?
Answer: I don't need to be afraid because God is with me and is able to protect me.

LET'S TALK ABOUT IT

What makes you feel scared? Maybe things like thunder, the dark, and getting shots. Why don't you need to be afraid of them anymore?

LET'S PRAY TOGETHER

Thank you, Lord Jesus, that you keep me safe. I'm so glad that you are always with me and that I don't have to be afraid. Amen.

God's Spirit

LET'S REMEMBER

The fruit of the Spirit is love…

GALATIANS 5:22

LET'S LISTEN

When someone asks Jesus into their life, the Holy Spirit begins to change them. God's Spirit begins to work inside the new Christian so that he or she will think and act like Jesus. When we let Jesus change us, we begin to love people more. Jesus takes away hate and envy. In its place, he gives us his love. Jesus said, "By this all will know that you are My disciples, if you have love for one another" (John 13:35).

LET'S ANSWER

Question: How will people know if you are a follower of Jesus?

Answer: People will know I am a follower of Jesus by my love for all people.

LET'S TALK ABOUT IT

Jesus gives love to his people to share with others. Who are some people with whom you want to share Jesus' love?

LET'S PRAY TOGETHER

Thank you, Father, for sending the Holy Spirit to help me think and act like Jesus. I want you to change me so that I can love people as you do. Amen.

LET'S REMEMBER

The fruit of the Spirit is love, joy...

GALATIANS 5:22

LET'S LISTEN

Christians have problems just like anyone else. But Christians have Jesus as their constant friend. He goes through our problems with us, and the Holy Spirit gives us joy even when we're in trouble.

Of course, there are times when we are sad, but even then, we can have joy because God works everything out for the best in the end: "All things work together for good to those who love God, to those who are called according to His purpose" (Romans 8:28).

LET'S ANSWER

Question: Why can Christians have joy even when things seem to go wrong?

Answer: Christians have joy even when things go wrong because God will work everything out in a good way in the end.

LET'S TALK ABOUT IT

What are some problems or troubles you have? Even in hard times, how can you have the joy of the Lord?

LET'S PRAY TOGETHER

Thank you, Lord Jesus, that even in times of trouble I can have your joy in my heart. It brings me joy just to think that I know you. Amen.

Peace

LET'S REMEMBER

The fruit of the Spirit is love, joy, peace...

GALATIANS 5:22

LET'S LISTEN

Most people want peaceful lives. We are at peace when we're not fighting with others. People often fight with each other because they are fighting against themselves. Those who don't know God don't have peace inside.

When we come to God by asking Jesus into our lives, we have peace with God. As we obey the Lord, the peace of God takes the place of our fears and makes us feel safe. Jesus promised his followers, "Peace I leave with you, My peace I give to you; not as the world gives do I give to you. Let not your heart be troubled, neither let it be afraid" (John 14:27).

LET'S ANSWER

Question: How do we live when we have peace?
Answer: When we have peace, we don't fight or argue with others. We are not afraid of God or angry with him.

Question: How do we make peace with God?
Answer: We make peace with God by asking Jesus to forgive our sins and be the Lord of our lives.

LET'S TALK ABOUT IT

What kind of peace does Jesus give us?

LET'S PRAY TOGETHER

Thank you, Lord Jesus, for giving me peace inside. Because of you, I have peace with you. Because I am at peace with you and with myself, I can be at peace with others. Amen.

LET'S REMEMBER

*The fruit of the Spirit
is love, joy, peace, longsuffering…*

GALATIANS 5:22

LET'S LISTEN

To be longsuffering means to be patient. To be patient means to trust God and to love others even when things don't go our way. Just think how patient God is with us. When we sin, he forgives us because he loves us. Even when we say we're sorry and then sin again, he keeps forgiving us.

Jesus lives inside those who have asked him into their lives. Now his Spirit within us makes us patient and understanding even when people do things that hurt us. The apostle Paul prayed that Christians would experience "patience and long-suffering with joy" (Colossians 1:11). Let's make that our prayer too.

LET'S ANSWER

Question: What does it mean to be longsuffering?
Answer: To be longsuffering means to be patient.

LET'S TALK ABOUT IT

Who are some people with whom you need to be patient?

LET'S PRAY TOGETHER

Lord Jesus, give me patience and longsuffering with joy. Thank you so much for being patient with me.
Amen.

LET'S REMEMBER

The fruit of the Spirit is love, joy, peace, longsuffering, kindness...

GALATIANS 5:22

LET'S LISTEN

Jesus was always kind to people who were hurting. He cared how they felt and wanted them to be happy and healthy. Since we want to be like Jesus, it is important that we care how others feel too. The Holy Spirit will help us to be kind by saying and doing what will make others glad and not saying things that will hurt others. The Bible says, "Be kind to one another, tenderhearted, forgiving one another, even as God in Christ forgave you" (Ephesians 4:32).

LET'S ANSWER

Question: How can you show kindness?
Answer: I can show kindness by saying and doing what will make others glad.

LET'S TALK ABOUT IT

Name someone who's in need of kindness. How can you show this person kindness today?

LET'S PRAY TOGETHER

Thank you, Jesus, for always being so kind to me. And thank you for helping me be kind to others. Amen.

LET'S REMEMBER

The fruit of the Spirit is love, joy, peace, longsuffering, kindness, goodness...

GALATIANS 5:22

LET'S LISTEN

Jesus is the only person who ever lived who was always truly good. But now his Spirit lives inside of us! So *his* goodness can be lived out through us! To be good means that we think, say, and do what pleases God. God's Spirit works in us to produce true goodness. The Bible says that those who trust Jesus as their Savior are "created in Christ Jesus for good works" (Ephesians 2:10).

LET'S ANSWER

Question: What is goodness?

Answer: Goodness is thinking, saying, and doing what pleases God.

LET'S TALK ABOUT IT

Who is the only person who ever lived who was always good? Does he now live inside of you?* Then his goodness is inside you, isn't it? Let's ask Jesus to let his goodness show through us.

LET'S PRAY TOGETHER

Lord Jesus, I'm so thankful you live inside of me since I've asked you into my life. I want you to live your life through mine. Thank you for the Holy Spirit, who works to make me like you. Amen.

*If your child has not yet prayed to receive Christ as Lord and Savior, you may want to reread "Jesus Is Lord and Savior" on page 72 or alter the prayer to better fit your child's spiritual condition.

LET'S REMEMBER

*The fruit of the Spirit is love, joy, peace,
longsuffering, kindness, goodness, faithfulness...*

GALATIANS 5:22

LET'S LISTEN

The Bible speaks many times about the need for Christians to be faithful. When someone is faithful, he can be trusted. When a person is faithful, she can be depended on. A faithful person can be counted on to do what he says he will do and to never turn away from what is true and right.

We should first be faithful to God. We show our faithfulness by how we live every day. If we learn to read the Bible and obey it, if we worship God and pray, if we tell others about Jesus, if we go to church whenever we can, then we are showing faithfulness to God.

We should also be faithful to those around us. We should always be loyal to our family and friends and never say anything unkind about them. When we tell someone we will do something for them, we should do it! This will show that we can be trusted and that we are faithful.

LET'S ANSWER

Question: How can you know if a person is faithful?

Answer: When a person is faithful, he can be trusted to do what he says he will do.

LET'S TALK ABOUT IT

The Bible says that God can be trusted to keep his promises (1 Thessalonians 5:24; 1 John 1:9). If we can trust God to keep his promises, shouldn't others be able to trust us as God's children to keep our promises? What are some ways that you can show faithfulness?

LET'S PRAY TOGETHER

Dear God, make me a faithful person by your Holy Spirit. I want you and other people to know I can be depended on to do those things I promise to do.
Amen.

LET'S REMEMBER

The fruit of the Spirit is love, joy, peace, longsuffering, kindness, goodness, faithfulness, gentleness...

GALATIANS 5:22–23

LET'S LISTEN

People are sometimes mean and cruel. They shout hurtful things and act unkindly. People will hurt others because they themselves have been hurt by others. When people are mean to us, we should not be mean to them. The Bible teaches us not to return evil for evil. Instead, we are to pay them back with a blessing (1 Peter 3:9). We should be gentle and try to understand that they are probably hurting inside. We always want to remember the Golden Rule that Jesus gave us: "Whatever you want men to do to you, do also to them" (Matthew 7:12). In other words, treat others the way you want to be treated. That's the best way to live!

LET'S ANSWER

Question: What is the Golden Rule?

Answer: The Golden Rule says, "Whatever you want men to do to you, do also to them" (Matthew 7:12).

LET'S TALK ABOUT IT

Can you think of someone who has been unkind to you? How should you act toward that person?

LET'S PRAY TOGETHER

Dear God, help me to always remember the Golden Rule and to live by what it says. Make me truly gentle with all people. Amen.

Self-Control

LET'S REMEMBER

The fruit of the Spirit is love, joy, peace,
longsuffering, kindness, goodness, faithfulness,
gentleness, self-control.

GALATIANS 5:22–23

LET'S LISTEN

Self-control means we are able to choose how we behave. If people have self-control, they choose not to pout or throw temper tantrums. They stop eating when they're no longer hungry, and when it's time to turn off the video games, they do so without getting upset. People who have self-control are not controlled by what they want. Instead, they choose to do what is right even when they may not feel like it.

We have been learning about the fruit that the Holy Spirit grows in our lives. Some people call the different parts of this fruit "virtues." That means that the Holy Spirit helps us live more and more like Jesus. And when Jesus is Lord of every part of our lives, we have self-control.

LET'S ANSWER

Question: What is self-control?
Answer: Self-control means I am able to control how I behave.

Question: How do you develop Christian virtues?
Answer: The Holy Spirit grows Christian virtues in me.

LET'S TALK ABOUT IT

Name a time or situation when it is difficult to control how you act. If you have given your life to Jesus, you can do what is right at those times even when you don't feel like it. Ask Jesus to give you the strength to think wisely and do the right thing.

LET'S PRAY TOGETHER

Lord Jesus, you know the times when I need self-control. I'm asking you now to be in charge in all those times. Thank you that your Spirit makes self-control grow in those people who love you. Amen.

How to Make
God Happy

Faith in God

LET'S REMEMBER

Without faith it is impossible to please Him.

HEBREWS 11:6

LET'S LISTEN

We become Christians by placing our faith in Jesus Christ. To have faith means to believe in something we can't see, touch, or hear and to know that what we believe is true. Faith is a gift that we can ask God to give us.

Christians show God that they have faith in him by trusting him and trusting what he says in his Word, the Bible. This pleases God. God is also pleased when we trust him to take care of us. He knows what is best for us. You can show your faith in God by praying to him, telling your friends about Jesus, obeying your parents, and doing whatever you know will please your Father in heaven.

LET'S ANSWER

Question: What does it mean to have faith in God?
Answer: To have faith in God means to believe in him even though I can't see him. I show faith in God when I believe what he says in his Word, the Bible, and act on it.

LET'S TALK ABOUT IT

What are some things you are believing God will do that haven't happened yet? Keep trusting God. Expect him to do big things! "Now faith is confidence in what we hope for and assurance about what we do not see" (Hebrews 11:1 NIV).

LET'S PRAY TOGETHER

Thank you, Lord Jesus, for the gift of faith in you. Please give me faith to always believe what you promise and to trust you to take care of me in the best way. Amen.

LET'S REMEMBER

As many as received Him, to them He gave the right to become children of God, to those who believe in His name.

JOHN 1:12

LET'S LISTEN

You have two families! You belong to the family you live with, and you also belong to the family of God if you have given your life to Jesus. God's family is made up of all those who have asked Jesus to be the Lord of their lives. The Bible says that God gave these people the right to become his children. Everyone who has received Jesus as Lord and Savior is a child of God.

God knows it is hard to live without a family. That's why he has given us a big family called "the church." When you spend time with other Christians, they are more than just your friends. They are also your sisters and brothers in Christ. We meet each week as the church to worship God together.

Other Christians can help you live for Jesus, and you can help them do the same. That's why it's important to be with other Christians. When Christians get together to talk about how wonderful Jesus is, the Bible calls this "fellowship."

LET'S ANSWER

Question: Why should we spend time with other Christians?
Answer: We should spend time with other Christians because Christians can help each other live for Jesus.

LET'S TALK ABOUT IT

Name some things we can do at church that help us grow as Christians.

LET'S PRAY TOGETHER

Dear God, I'm glad to be part of your wonderful family. Thank you for the chance to meet together with other Christians to worship you and to learn how we can serve you better. Amen.

LET'S REMEMBER

Whatever you ask in My name, that I will do, that the Father may be glorified in the Son.

JOHN 14:13

LET'S LISTEN

Prayer is talking to God. God loves for us to come to him with all of our needs, joys, secrets, and dreams. We can talk to him about anything. He is always ready to listen to you.

We are to pray in Jesus' name. This means we can ask for things from God as though Jesus himself were asking, so we must always remember to ask for things that would please Jesus. When he answers our prayers, we see his power at work.

LET'S ANSWER

Question: What is prayer?
Answer: Prayer is talking to God.

Question: In whose name are you to pray?
Answer: I am to pray in the name of Jesus.

LET'S TALK ABOUT IT

Look again at the great promise Jesus made in John 14:13. What is something that will please God that hasn't happened yet? Ask God to make it happen in Jesus' name.

LET'S PRAY TOGETHER

Dear God, I'm glad I can come straight to you because Jesus has opened the way. I'm asking you now to [place your request here]. I know that when you answer this request it will bring glory to you. I ask you to answer my prayer because I am praying in Jesus' name. Amen.

LET'S REMEMBER

All Scripture is given by inspiration of God.

2 TIMOTHY 3:16

LET'S LISTEN

God has written you a love letter! God's love letter to you is the Bible. In the Bible we find out how very much God loves us. We discover that God loves us so much he sent Jesus, his Son, to die for us. The Bible tells us what God is like and how we can know him and honor him.

The Bible is God's Word, and God cannot lie (Titus 1:2; Hebrews 6:18). Throughout its history, the church has believed the Bible is true. Though some people have tried to prove there are mistakes in the Bible, they have never found even one! Because God loves us, he has given us a book we can trust. It is his love letter to his children and his message to all the world.

LET'S ANSWER

Question: What does the Bible tell us?
Answer: The Bible tells us what God is like, how we can know him, and how we can live for him.

LET'S TALK ABOUT IT

Today we send messages to others in many ways. Have you received a message from someone? God has sent you a special message called the Bible. He wants you to listen carefully to what he wrote to you. When we obey what the Bible teaches, our lives are full of joy.

LET'S PRAY TOGETHER

*Thank you, God, for your Holy Word, the Bible.
Teach me to respect, love, and obey your Word.
In Jesus' name. Amen.*

LET'S REMEMBER

Follow Me, and I will make you fishers of men.

MATTHEW 4:19

LET'S LISTEN

If we know Jesus, we will want others to know him too. The good news about him is too wonderful to keep to ourselves. When we tell others about Jesus, we feel a special joy inside. What could be more exciting than bringing someone else to Jesus so they can know him too! Jesus says that if we follow him, we will learn how to "fish" for people. That means we will tell others about him and let him draw people to him.

The Bible says, "For I am not ashamed of the gospel of Christ, for it is the power of God to salvation for everyone who believes" (Romans 1:16). We should never be ashamed of the good news about Jesus. It's the best news the world will ever hear. How happy we are when we tell others about Jesus!

LET'S ANSWER

Question: If you follow Jesus, what will you become?

Answer: If I follow Jesus, I will become a "fisher of men" by telling others about Jesus.

LET'S TALK ABOUT IT

Who are some people you know who need to hear the good news about Jesus? When will you tell them about him?

LET'S PRAY TOGETHER

Thank you, Jesus, for letting me tell others about you. I'm glad that I can tell people the best news they will ever hear. Help me never to be afraid to talk to my friends about you. In Jesus' name. Amen.

How to Live

The Poor in Spirit

LET'S REMEMBER

Blessed are the poor in spirit,
for theirs is the kingdom of heaven.

MATTHEW 5:3

LET'S LISTEN

One day Jesus taught a lot of people who gathered around him on a mountainside. He taught them that the purpose of their lives was to please God. He showed them how to have a blessed life. When Jesus said we would be blessed if we followed his teachings, he meant that we would be truly happy if we do what he says.

He said first, "Blessed [or happy] are the poor in spirit, for theirs is the kingdom of heaven." This means that those people who realize they are not good enough to come to God on their own are happy. Why? Because they are the only ones who rely on Jesus to bring them to God. They will live in the kingdom of heaven.

LET'S ANSWER

Question: Is anyone good enough to get to heaven on their own?

Answer: No one is good enough to get to heaven on their own. We must trust in Jesus to bring us to God and to heaven.

LET'S TALK ABOUT IT

Some people think they're good enough to come to God without believing in Jesus. We call this "spiritual pride," which is sort of like bragging or believing that we're better than we really are. Jesus taught us to be "poor in spirit," to realize that we must have his goodness in us. Have you come to God as someone who is poor in spirit?

LET'S PRAY TOGETHER

Dear God, I know I'm not good enough to come live with you in heaven. But I'm glad you will accept me because I have received Jesus, your Son. I believe that his blood is the full payment for all my sins. Help me always to know my need of you so I can be happy and receive your true riches. In Jesus' name. Amen.

LET'S REMEMBER

Blessed are those who mourn,
for they shall be comforted.

MATTHEW 5:4

LET'S LISTEN

Think of this! Jesus said that people who are sad can be blessed and happy. It is a good thing to be sad if we are sad about the things that make God sad. A man with a big heart for people who are hurting once prayed, "Let my heart be broken by the things that break the heart of God."*

Sad things happen in every person's life. But when we are sad, Jesus is very close to us. "The Lord is near to those who have a broken heart" (Psalm 34:18). He will comfort us when we are sad. Many of those who are sad now will rejoice in the future, especially in heaven.

LET'S ANSWER

Question: When is a special time that Jesus is close to us?

Answer: Jesus is close to us when we're sad.

LET'S TALK ABOUT IT

Do you remember a sad time in your life? Jesus is there to comfort you and be close to you when your heart hurts.

LET'S PRAY TOGETHER

Thank you, Lord Jesus, that you don't leave your children sad forever. You turn their sadness into joy. Amen.

---

*The late Bob Pierce, founder of World Vision and Samaritan's Purse

LET'S REMEMBER

*Blessed are the meek,
for they shall inherit the earth.*

MATTHEW 5:5

LET'S LISTEN

We've already learned that when we are gentle
people, we obey the Golden Rule. That rule,
given by Jesus, says, "Whatever you want men
to do to you, do also to them" (Matthew 7:12).
Sadly, some people choose not to be gentle and to
disobey the Golden Rule. They believe it is okay
to fight and be mean if that's what it takes to get
their own way.

But we know better. Jesus promises that one
day the earth will belong to those who are gentle
and who care about others. That's a present worth
waiting for!

LET'S ANSWER

Question: What will be the big prize for those who are gentle?

Answer: One day the earth will belong to those who are gentle.

LET'S PRAY TOGETHER

Thank you, Lord, for the great future I have with you! Teach me to be gentle so that I may one day inherit the earth. In Jesus' name. Amen.

Those Who Hunger for Righteousness

LET'S REMEMBER

Blessed are those who hunger and thirst for righteousness, for they shall be filled.

MATTHEW 5:6

LET'S LISTEN

When we're hungry, we want food. When we're thirsty, we want water. All people desire food and water each day, and we need them to live. We should also want to please God just as much as a hungry, thirsty child wants food and water. That's what it means to hunger and thirst after righteousness. It means we always want to please God in what we say, think, and do.

We can ask God to give us this desire. If you have that hunger, it means you want to please God in all that you think, say, and do. When we are filled with the Holy Spirit, we have God's power to live the kind of life that pleases him.

LET'S ANSWER

Question: What does it mean to hunger and thirst for righteousness?

Answer: To hunger and thirst for righteousness means to desire to please God in all that I think, say, and do.

LET'S TALK ABOUT IT

Have you ever played for a long time and then felt hungry or thirsty? We should also be "hungry" to please God in everything we think, say, and do. What are some ways you can please God?

LET'S PRAY TOGETHER

Dear God, I want to please you with all of my heart. Fill me with your Holy Spirit so I can have power to live a life that pleases you. In Jesus' name. Amen.

The Merciful

LET'S REMEMBER

Blessed are the merciful,
for they shall obtain mercy.

MATTHEW 5:7

LET'S LISTEN

"He ought to be punished!" Have you ever heard anyone say that? Maybe a boy or girl made a poor choice and deserves punishment. But how beautiful it is when we are kind and show mercy to that child. To show mercy means not punishing someone even if they made a poor choice. Instead, we choose to forgive that person from our heart.

It's important we remember that we should have been punished for going our own way instead of God's way. But Jesus had mercy on us and took the punishment himself! Just think how much he loves us. Since Jesus showed mercy to us, we should show mercy to others. If we show mercy to others now, we will receive mercy later.

LET'S ANSWER

Question: What is the reward for showing mercy to others?

Answer: If I show mercy toward others, God will show mercy to me.

LET'S TALK ABOUT IT

Whom can you show mercy to right now?

LET'S PRAY TOGETHER

Lord Jesus, you have been so full of mercy to me. You have forgiven all my sins and taken all my punishment. Help me now to be merciful to others. I ask this in your name. Amen.

The Pure in Heart

Blessed are the pure in heart,
for they shall see God.

MATTHEW 5:8

LET'S LISTEN

The prophet Jeremiah said, "The heart is deceitful above all things, and desperately wicked (Jeremiah 17:9). Our hearts can play tricks on us. Sometimes we think it is better to do what is wrong than to do what God says. Evil ways and evil thoughts are natural when a person doesn't know Jesus. And even those who love Jesus sometimes think or do wrong things. But they can and will change because Jesus lives in them.

After King David had sinned, he prayed, "Create in me a clean heart, O God, and renew a steadfast spirit within me" (Psalm 51:10). God can give you a pure heart. When Jesus comes into your life, he makes your heart—that secret part of you that only God can see—clean and pure. If Jesus is in your life, then you will one day see God the Father.

LET'S ANSWER

Question: Who can make your heart clean and pure?

Answer: Jesus can make my heart clean and pure.

LET'S TALK ABOUT IT

Why does your heart need to be made new by Jesus? What does it mean when the Bible says our hearts are deceitful and wicked?

LET'S PRAY TOGETHER

Dear God, my prayer is the same as King David's prayer of long ago. "Create in me a clean heart, O God, and renew a steadfast spirit within me." In Jesus' name. Amen.

LET'S REMEMBER

Blessed are the peacemakers,
for they shall be called sons of God.

MATTHEW 5:9

LET'S LISTEN

A peacemaker is someone who tries to turn enemies into friends. It is not always an easy job. Sometimes people who are angry at each other will become angry at a peacemaker too. This is what happened to Jesus, the Prince of Peace.

Our Bible verse promises that peacemakers will be called sons of God. Children of God are those who have Jesus living inside of them. We have already learned that Jesus brings peace and happiness into our lives. As children of God, we want others to know this peace and happiness too. God has given us a special job of bringing peace between people who don't like each other. That's our job: turning enemies into friends!

LET'S ANSWER

Question: What is the reward given to peacemakers?

Answer: Peacemakers will be called sons of God.

LET'S TALK ABOUT IT

Can you think of anyone you know who is angry with someone else? What can you do to help them become friends?

LET'S PRAY TOGETHER

Dear God, let people know that I belong to you because I work to turn enemies into friends. In Jesus' name. Amen.

LET'S REMEMBER

Blessed are those who are persecuted for righteousness' sake, for theirs is the kingdom of heaven.

MATTHEW 5:10

LET'S LISTEN

Christians are sometimes called to suffer for the name of Jesus. Peter, one of Jesus' disciples, said, "For to this you were called, because Christ also suffered for us, leaving us an example, that you should follow His steps" (1 Peter 2:21). It is a high honor to hurt for Christ and the gospel. It might not be a physical pain. Some Christians lose friends when they follow Jesus. Some Christians are laughed at. Others are cursed or bullied.

You will be called to hurt for Jesus in some way someday. Then you will know what it means to be "persecuted for righteousness' sake." You never need to be afraid of this. Those who suffer for Jesus know that he is with them. And remember the reward: "For theirs is the kingdom of heaven."

LET'S ANSWER

Question: What is the reward for those who are persecuted for righteousness' sake?

Answer: The reward for those who are persecuted for Jesus is the kingdom of heaven.

LET'S TALK ABOUT IT

Why should we never be afraid to suffer for Jesus? How can we be prepared to suffer for Jesus?

LET'S PRAY TOGETHER

Dear God, I know it is an honor to suffer for you and your cause. Help me never to be afraid to live for you, whatever the cost. Help me never to be ashamed of you. I love you, Lord. Keep me true to you all the days of my life. In Jesus' name. Amen.

Important
Words

Repentance

LET'S REMEMBER

Repent, and believe in the gospel.

MARK 1:15

LET'S LISTEN

Sin is anything in our lives that does not please God. Sin is not caring about what God wants and living just to please ourselves. When a person repents, he stops living for himself and starts living for God. He changes his mind about the way he should live.

Before we can really live as God desires, we must repent. This means we must stop living just to please ourselves. When we repent, we change our mind and start thinking God's way. We turn around and go toward God. Then we will want to think and do only what will make God happy.

LET'S ANSWER

Question: What happens when you repent?

Answer: When I repent, I stop living just to please myself and start living to please God. I turn from any bad things I am doing. I change my mind about what I am doing, and I go God's way.

LET'S TALK ABOUT IT

What are some thoughts or actions from which you should turn away?

LET'S PRAY TOGETHER

Dear God, I turn from anything in my life that doesn't please you. I change my mind and want to go your way. I turn to you and ask you to help me live in a way that pleases you. In Jesus' name. Amen.

LET'S REMEMBER

Whoever calls on the name of the Lord shall be saved.

Romans 10:13

LET'S LISTEN

Our greatest need is for salvation. When someone asks God to forgive him for his sins and gives his life to Jesus, that person is "saved." First, he is saved from being punished for his sins. Punishment for sins would have put us in a place far from God forever after we die. But we are saved from that penalty, thanks to Jesus. "For God so loved the world that He gave His only begotten Son, that whoever believes in Him should not perish but have everlasting life" (John 3:16). If Jesus lives inside of us, we want to please God.

A believer in Jesus is also saved from wasting his life doing things that do not bring him peace inside. But once we are saved, we can live lives that please God and have his peace in us.

LET'S ANSWER

Question: What are believers in Jesus saved from?
Answer: Believers in Jesus are saved from God's judgment for their sins. Jesus took the punishment for us.

Question: What are believers in Jesus able to do once they are saved from God's judgment?
Answer: Believers in Jesus can learn to live lives that please God because the Holy Spirit will help them.

LET'S TALK ABOUT IT

The word *salvation* means "to be rescued out of danger." What danger were we in before Jesus came into our lives?

LET'S PRAY TOGETHER

Thank you, Jesus, for taking the punishment for my sins when you died on the cross. God's judgment that should have come to me instead fell on you, Lord, because you paid for my sins. Help me to live a life that makes you happy. In Jesus' name. Amen.

Reverence

LET'S REMEMBER

God is greatly to be feared in the assembly of the saints, and to be held in reverence by all those who are around Him.

PSALM 89:7

LET'S LISTEN

To revere God means to have respect for his power, his love, and his name. When the Bible tells us to fear God, it means we are to give God the highest respect and honor as our heavenly Father.

God is our Creator, and he has the power to do anything. He can create storms and stop them. He can create life and take it away. When we revere God, we are amazed by his wonderful acts. We should never take his name lightly or joke about him. We bow before him in worship, love, and obedience.

LET'S ANSWER

Question: What does it mean to revere God?

Answer: To revere God means to have a great respect for his power, his love, and his name. We honor him as our Creator, Redeemer, healer, and friend.

LET'S TALK ABOUT IT

What are some ways you can show reverence for God?

LET'S PRAY TOGETHER

Dear God, I bow in reverence before you. I praise you for your power, your love, and your name. I love you, and I honor you. In Jesus' name. Amen.

Obedience

LET'S REMEMBER

Children, obey your parents in the Lord,
for this is right.

<small>EPHESIANS 6:1</small>

LET'S LISTEN

God has placed people in our lives whom we are to obey. He has done this because he loves us. These people protect us, teach us, and help us. Our parents, grandparents, teachers, and pastors are all gifts to us from God.

When we obey, we do what we are told to do. When we do this for the Lord, we show Jesus that we want to obey his Word, the Bible. Jesus said, "If you love Me, keep My commandments" (John 14:15). We should always obey what God says in his Word. And there is a special promise for those who obey their parents. The Bible says they will have a long, happy life (Ephesians 6:1–3).

LET'S ANSWER

Question: What does the Bible promise if you obey your parents?

Answer: If I obey my parents, I will have a long, happy life.

LET'S TALK ABOUT IT

Name three people in your life whom you should obey. What one book should you always obey?

LET'S PRAY TOGETHER

Dear Lord, I pray that I will obey those you have placed over me to protect and help me. May I always obey your Holy Word, the Bible. In Jesus' name. Amen.

LET'S REMEMBER

Be kind to one another, tenderhearted, forgiving one another, even as God in Christ forgave you.

Ephesians 4:32

LET'S LISTEN

What do you do when someone bullies you? Do you become angry and look for a way to be mean to them? People who refuse to forgive others can become hateful because their anger builds up inside them. Hateful people are never fun to be around. Some people even get sick because they won't forgive those who hurt them. When we don't forgive others, we can't become good friends with Jesus.

If you don't forgive when others treat you unfairly, then you become angry. You won't have peace, and you won't be fun to be around. We're never truly happy when we aren't close to Jesus. When we desire to please him, then we are truly happy. Jesus has forgiven us for all our sins. Since he forgave us, we should forgive others.

LET'S ANSWER

Question: Why should you forgive others?
Answer: I should forgive others because Jesus has forgiven me.

LET'S TALK ABOUT IT

Is there someone who has hurt you whom you need to forgive?

LET'S PRAY TOGETHER

Thank you, Father, for forgiving me of all my sins against you. Just as you have forgiven me for hurting you, I now forgive all those who have hurt me. Help me always to forgive quickly when I am wronged. In Jesus' name. Amen.

Love

LET'S REMEMBER

All will know that you are My disciples,
if you have love for one another.

JOHN 13:35

LET'S LISTEN

People will know that we are Jesus' followers, his disciples, if we love one another. Everything about us should show love.

The apostle Paul told us what this love of God is like. "Love suffers long and is kind; love does not envy; love does not parade itself, is not puffed up; does not behave rudely, does not seek its own, is not provoked, thinks no evil; does not rejoice in iniquity, but rejoices in the truth; bears all things, believes all things, hopes all things, endures all things. Love never fails" (1 Corinthians 13:4–8). When people see that kind of love in us, they will know we are true followers of Jesus.

LET'S ANSWER

Question: How will others know that you are following Jesus?

Answer: Others will know I am following Jesus if I show love for others.

LET'S TALK ABOUT IT

What are some ways you can show love to others? What first step of love will you take today?

LET'S PRAY TOGETHER

Dear God, help me to love others as you do. Then everyone will know I am a follower of Jesus. In his name. Amen.

Disciple

LET'S REMEMBER

By this My Father is glorified, that you bear much fruit; so you will be My disciples.

JOHN 15:8

LET'S LISTEN

A disciple is a person who follows Jesus and his teachings. A disciple is also a learner. We prove we are his followers by producing much fruit for his glory. But what does it mean to produce or bear fruit for God?

To begin with, you can learn more and more about Jesus and his ways. You can do this by talking to God in prayer. You can also listen to God's Word, the Bible. You can worship God with other followers of Jesus. The character of Jesus will be seen in you, and that will glorify God!

Then you can produce fruit by telling others the good news about Jesus and showing them how to get close to God. This will be a harvest of new believers.

LET'S ANSWER

Question: What does it mean to be a disciple of Jesus?

Answer: Being a disciple means that I am following Jesus and learning more about him and his ways. I prove I am following him by letting the Holy Spirit produce fruit in my life.

LET'S TALK ABOUT IT

Name two things we can do to tie in closer to Jesus and learn more of him and his ways.

LET'S PRAY TOGETHER

Dear God, help me to be a good follower of Jesus and produce much fruit. Help me to always be learning more about him and his ways.
In his name. Amen.

LET'S REMEMBER

The disciples were first called Christians in Antioch.

ACTS 11:26

LET'S LISTEN

A person is not a Christian because he goes to church or is a church member. A person is not a Christian because he has been baptized or christened. A person is not a Christian because he does kind deeds. Christians do all these things, but that is not what makes a person a Christian.

A Christian is a person who has Jesus Christ living inside of him. If you can truly say that you have turned away from your sins and Jesus is now Lord of your life, and if you believe God raised Jesus from the dead, then you are a Christian, and Jesus lives in you: "If you confess with your mouth the Lord Jesus and believe in your heart that God has raised Him from the dead, you will be saved" (Romans 10:9).

LET'S ANSWER

Question: What is a Christian?

Answer: A Christian is someone who has Jesus living inside of him.

LET'S TALK ABOUT IT

When people look at you, how can they tell that you are a Christian?

LET'S PRAY TOGETHER

Lord Jesus, thank you for living inside of me. Teach me to live in such a way that people will know that I belong to you. In your name. Amen.

Victory

LET'S REMEMBER

Thanks be to God, who gives us the victory through our Lord Jesus Christ.

1 Corinthians 15:57

LET'S LISTEN

Sometimes people who are against God are against us too. Many of us feel a fight inside of us to choose God's way instead of our own way. Still, we can win with joy in our hearts because Jesus has won against all his enemies: "His divine power has given us everything we need for a godly life through the knowledge of him who called us" (2 Peter 1:3 NIV).

Even during tough times, God is for you: "For I know the thoughts that I think toward you, says the Lord, thoughts of peace and not of evil, to give you a future and a hope" (Jeremiah 29:11).

In the end, Jesus wins. He will rule in love over everything! The biggest win of all will be to hear Jesus say to you, "Well done, good and faithful servant; you were faithful over a few

things, I will make you ruler over many things.
Enter into the joy of your lord" (Matthew 25:21).
Let's always live for Jesus and spread his love
everywhere!

LET'S ANSWER

Question: Who has overcome the world?
Answer: Jesus has overcome the world.

Question: Who is the "greater One" who lives in
you?
Answer: Jesus lives in me, and he is greater than
any problem I face.

LET'S TALK ABOUT IT

How can we win our spiritual battles?

LET'S PRAY TOGETHER

I praise you, Lord Jesus, because you are greater
than any problem I face. You have good plans for
my future. I'm thankful that you will always be
with me and, as I trust you, you will always lead
me to victory. Amen.

ACKNOWLEDGMENTS

Both of us were privileged to be raised in Christian homes by parents who loved Jesus and lived Christ-honoring lives. We're forever grateful to them for sharing the Bible's truth with us. This book is an expression of our appreciation.

We're grateful to Carlton Garborg and the entire team at BroadStreet Publishing for believing in this project. Earlier editions have helped thousands of Christian families, and we're thankful that this resource is available once again to encourage family time with God.

Finally, we're deeply grateful for a group of friends who literally prayed this book into existence. Your faith is now made sight.

What Christians Believe

LET'S REMEMBER

I believe in God, the Father almighty, Creator of heaven and earth. I believe in Jesus Christ, God's only Son, our Lord, who was conceived by the Holy Spirit, born of the Virgin Mary, suffered under Pontius Pilate, was crucified, dead, and was buried; he descended into hell. The third day he rose again; he ascended into heaven and is seated at the right hand of the Father, from there he will come again to judge the living and the dead. I believe in the Holy Spirit, the holy catholic* church, the communion of saints, the forgiveness of sins, the resurrection of the body, and the life everlasting. Amen.

What we have just read is known as the Apostles' Creed. When we recite a creed, we say what we believe and know to be true. Long ago, Christians decided they should write down their most important beliefs. They did this to help them stay away from wrong teachings. Through most of the history of Christianity, Christians have been reciting this creed to remind them of the great treasure of their faith in Jesus Christ.

Today we are joined in faith with all those who have believed in Jesus throughout history. It is an honor to be part of that large group of people through the centuries who belong to Jesus. They are our brothers and sisters in Christ. Let's recite the Apostles' Creed again.

LET'S ANSWER

Question: What is the Apostles' Creed?
Answer: The Apostles' Creed is a statement of some of the most important beliefs and truths we share with other Christians around the world.

LET'S TALK ABOUT IT

Are there words or ideas in this creed you don't understand? Let's talk about what they mean.

LET'S PRAY TOGETHER

Thank you, Father, that the truth about you and the truth about your Son, the Lord Jesus, never changes. I'm glad my faith rests on facts that have always been true and always will be. Help me to always stand boldly for your truth and share my faith in you with love and joy. Amen.

---

*That is, the true Christian church of all times and all places.

The Creation

Genesis 1:1–2:3

The Great Flood

Genesis 6:14–7:24

Joseph's Beautiful Coat

Genesis 37:1–34

Baby Moses

Exodus 1:22–2:10

Joshua and the Battle of Jericho

Joshua 6:1–20

Samson Forgets His Vow

Judges 16:4–30

Young Samuel and God's Voice

1 Samuel 3

David and Goliath

1 Samuel 17

The Fiery Furnace

Daniel 3

ABOUT THE AUTHORS

David and Naomi Shibley have been married since 1972. In 1990, they founded Global Advance to empower leaders worldwide to disciple their nations for Christ. Visit globaladvance.org to learn more.

The Shibleys have two adult sons, two wonderful daughters-in-law, and five grandchildren. Both sons and their families serve Jesus.